MW01127498

MIRACLE
ON
THE
PRAIRIE

**Building the Church of
St. Paul, Apostle of the Nations**
at
Marty, South Dakota, 1942

by

Mary Eisenman Carson

Copyright © 2008 by Mary Eisenman Carson

ISBN 0-7414-4820-3

1. Yankton Sioux Indians, history, landmark, shrine, stonework.

2. St. Paul's Mission, Marty, South Dakota

BOOK FORMATTED by Alfred Tietjen of Fusion Studios, Seattle, Washington, U.S.A.

COVER DESIGNED by Author.

Published by:

INFINITY
PUBLISHING.COM

1094 New DeHaven Street, Suite 100
West Conshohocken, PA 19428-2713
Info@buybooksontheweb.com
www.buybooksontheweb.com
Toll-free (877) BUY BOOK
Local Phone (610) 941-9999
Fax (610) 941-9959

Printed in the United States of America

Printed on Recycled Paper

Published May 2008

Acknowledgements

Among many who offered support in this history, this author owes thanks to:

Mark Thiel in the Department of Special Collections and University Archives, Marquette University, Milwaukee, Wisconsin, for access to Marty photos that I had identified, catalogued and taken to Milwaukee in 1983 under the title "Saint Paul's Mission Collection." This at the request of the Mission.

To the Oblate Sisters of the Blessed Sacrament at Marty, tireless for remembering and digging to add to this history.

To Helen Foster Eisenman, the wife of my brother Joseph, for invaluable help scanning other photos and aligning all.

To my son Paul, for Guardian Angel, over-the-shoulder computer help and encouragement.

To Monsignor Paul A. Lenz, longtime Bureau of Catholic Indian Missions director, for his enduring interest in Native American history, and his encouragement on all four of my books on the Yankton Sioux tribe.

PHOTO CREDITS

FRONT COVER— Sanctuary photo: PHOTOGRAPHY BY DENELLE, Pickstown, South Dakota. (See Appendix No. 8, p. 83, for a detailed description of this mural.)

Dakota Sioux Designs: Photo by Paul Thomas Carson, Seattle, Washington [beaded coin purse given to author in the 1930s].

BACK COVER— Stained glass window photo: PHOTOGRAPHY BY DENELLE, Pickstown, South Dakota.

EFC---Eisenman Family Collection.

Photos not otherwise credited are from:

Saint Paul Mission Collection, Department of Special Collections and University Archives, Marquette University, Milwaukee, Wisconsin.

Contents

Introduction

Miracle on the Prairie: Building St. Paul Apostle of the Nations Church at Marty, South Dakota, 1942, is an amazing story of faith and determination among the Yankton Sioux people, authored by one who had witnessed many of the events. The story begins with the prayers, hopes, and dreams of the Yankton ancestors – Chief Padanniapapi (Old Strike), Chief Mahpiyato (Blue Cloud, or William Bean), Grandma Osotewin (Smoke Woman or Mary White Tallow), and many others – and it continues by chronicling the planning, organizing, and construction of a beautiful Christian house of worship and school, amid years of hardship, struggles, and sheer determination under the capable leadership of Benedictine Father Sylvester Eisenman.

The Yankton (*iha^{n}ke* 'end,' *to^n'wa^n* 'village 'end village') are one of seven primary divisions of the Dakota or Sioux Indians. By the early 18th century, they had established their homeland on the east bank of the Missouri River – near present-day Sioux City, Iowa. But they resided here vulnerable and without firearms, after Ojibwa with firearms had driven them out of the Minnesota lake region.

Consequently, they welcomed Lewis & Clark and Father Pierre-Jean De Smet, S.J. They took to heart their messages of peace and hope and they trusted DeSmet and the Blackrobes who followed. By treaty in 1858, the Yankton ceded all lands except a reservation on the north bank of Missouri River, and under Padanniappi, they maintained neutrality during the 1862 Dakota War and succeeded in saving the lives of hundreds of American settlers.

Meanwhile, the Yankton were plagued by European diseases, drought, poverty, and misery as their population imploded and declined rapidly from over 3,000 to nearly half its former size. It was to these people that Father Sylvester dedicated himself when he first came to Marty in 1918, and then secured a Post Office named in honor of the Benedictine Martin Marty, the first bishop of Dakota Territory.

Father Sylvester took to heart the Yankton dream for a church and school of-their-own. In so doing, he made a life-long commitment – he learned their native Dakota language, he laid plans, and he recruited skilled family members, friends, and Saint Katharine Drexel with her teaching Sisters of the Blessed Sacrament. Together, this collaborative effort of Yankton Sioux and friends labored in a noble cause. They gathered stones, poured concrete, erected steel and arches, and adorned the church with Yankton artwork, which, in 1942, culminated with the consecration of St. Paul the Apostle Church, a legacy today that inspires the future.

—Mark G. Thiel, CA, Archivist
Marquette University, Milwaukee, Wisconsin

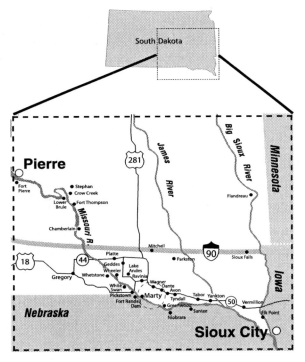

Vicinity of Marty, South Dakota

Preface

"Cowboy and Indian" days are gone. Embracing the nascent movie industry, the audience roared when the Indians "bit the dust." On a vacant lot in Indianapolis, my own mother in her teens pounded the piano keyboard beneath an outdoor silent screen, with crescendos to match the action: flying hooves, lariats, arrows.

By contrast, early 21st Century media prefer American Indian historic surroundings, customs, feelings of bravery, love of family, grief and joy.

Colleges maintain Departments of American Indian Affairs. Universities offer study-experience on Reservations. Native American scholarships increase.

In the process, researchers discover how pioneering missionaries of many faiths managed to prepare their students for professions and trades, with Indian surnames making their mark in succeeding generations.

Almost overlooked, however, is how whole families were saved from dying out. The steady burden raising funds to sustain schools and provide basic necessities of life on the Reservations is a record largely unappreciated and undocumented. But today's historians delight to learn how missionaries left records of ancestral tribes, beginning with French Jesuits in the 1600s on the St. Lawrence River, and enduring throughout the 20th century with the Yanktons.

Miracle On The Prairie attempts to capture the drama and mystery behind one enigmatic shrine on Dakota's vast plain. It is meant to prove that sacrifice of self and vision of faith cast in brotherly love—in any age—is noble.

—Mary Elizabeth Eisenman Carson, 2008

DEDICATED TO

*Chief Struck By The Ree, or Padanniapapi, who
with compelling foresight in 1844, at age 40, sued
for a Blackrobe with the faith in Jesus Christ to
come and school his tribe, the Yankton Sioux.*

*And to the ardent descendants of "Old Strike"
and their countless friends across the U. S. who
saw their dream culminate in this enduring
shrine.*

MIRACLE ON THE PRAIRIE

Building the Church of St. Paul,
Apostle of the Nations
at Marty, South Dakota, 1942

W hat is this surprising sight far out on the South Dakota prairie, the gleaming white steeple jutting up 167 feet from an acreage of old-growth trees on a once treeless expanse?

Is it a monument, a shrine, or a natural wonder? Or all three? Every year at the Lincoln Memorial and the Vietnam Wall, millions feel a surge of patriotism—or they sympathize with an ancient race at the Crazy Horse Monument. They experience God's majesty at Niagara Falls, or feel a stab in the heart on walking the Vicksburg Battleground beside the Mississippi where, it so happened, this author lost a Great Great Uncle Henry Hulsman.

Behind every shrine or monument lies a three-fold story: who conceived the idea; who carried it out; and what heroic hardships of weather, worker and cost affected its birth. We can but gaze in amazement.

Today we ask, "How did this towering landmark arise in the center of the isolated Yankton Sioux Reservation at Marty, South Dakota, the home of St. Paul's Mission in Charles Mix County?" The area now in 2008 includes—besides the Mission Church—the Yankton Sioux Tribal Headquarters, and thriving Marty Indian School.

SOUTH DAKOTA HISTORICAL MARKER AT MARTY. *[Birth date of Father Sylvester should read 1891.] A passing journalist called Marty* **"The Miracle on the Prairie."** (To read the text of this monument, see Appendix No.1, page 80.)

What strands of distant culture came together long ago in this place on the Great Plains? Surprising stories emerge from the past, but new ones complicate the mystery of this appealing 1942 shrine. For answers, we begin with the more recent tales:

> Old-timers still alive in 2008 like to claim: "I built the church at Marty." This booklet, MIRACLE ON THE PRAIRIE, will prove theirs is no idle boast. Not even world cathedrals can list young and old—skilled and unskilled—in their labor force, without a master builder at the helm. Within these pages a tale of homespun, rock-bottom toil and ingenuity will uncover the faces and forces that placed Marty's imposing church on this spot. Thus, Marty graduates near and far, with cohorts on the Reservation, can still boast of their novel role in building the 1942 church of St. Paul Apostle of the Nations, a gift for ensuing generations.

Monument to Fortitude of the Old Chiefs

Inside a collection of old letters and snapshots lie poignant details on the building of this unique monument. A monument it is, to faith and sacrifice, and to the persistence of a long line of Yankton Sioux leaders, handsome young men in their Smithsonian portraits, notably Little Swan, Feather in the Ear, Medicine Cow, Jumping Thunder, and Chief Struck by the Ree. Perhaps the latter, called "Old Strike" or Padanniapapi, was the most impassioned. In 1866 he addressed a message to the U. S. Government: "I have made up my mind on this subject twenty-two years ago. I wish to put the instruction of the youth of my tribe into the hands of the Blackrobes. I consider them alone the depositaries of the ancient and true faith of Jesus Christ, and we are free to hear and follow them. My mind is made up." The revered chief won the admiration of Jesuit Father Pierre-Jean DeSmet, who wrote, on one of his early 1830s journeys to the Western tribes: "In my long experience with Indians, I have never seen so durable and admirable a persistency."

The latest of Yanktons to wait long years was Mahpiyato, Chief Blue Cloud*, or William Bean. The Chief's final and deathbed wish for a school came on Father Sylvester's first visit to the Yanktons September 8, 1918. Baptized by Father DeSmet, Mahpiyato died at 85 without seeing the dream realized, though he left descendants with zeal equal to his own.

(* Blue Cloud means a Light Rain cloud, a Blessing cloud.)

THE SAGA OF THE YANKTON CHIEFS' INSISTENT REQUESTS, with a detailed early history of the tribe, including early struggles at Marty, are found in this author's first three books:

Blackrobe for the Yankton Sioux: Fr. Sylvester Eisenman, O.S.B. (1891-1948), published 1989.

American Indian Legends of the Holy Man, 2000.

8th Landing: The Yankton Sioux Meet Lewis And Clark, 2005

Two Builder Brothers

Epochal decades of drought, dust, grasshoppers, Great Depression, isolation and World War II shortages set the background. But Providence provided two inspired leaders, backed by a remote army of donors across America whose sympathies for the abandoned Dakota Indians hung on a small newsletter, *The Little Bronzed Angel*, coming from Marty every month. Through the deep Depression, the "benefactors" kept the sacrificial envelopes coming. The missionary, Father Sylvester, had an uncanny knack for gathering lists of names from random phone books.

This short history tells the improbable story of Father Sylvester Eisenman, his builder-brother Leonard, and the untraditional heroes of this Marty shrine.

Above - **THE BROTHER OF FATHER SYLVESTER**, *Leonard John Eisenman, Sr. His letters and other sources give an inside clue to the building of this imposing temple.* ---EFC

Left - **FATHER SYLVESTER EISENMAN, O.S.B.** *[Order of St. Benedict]* ---EFC

Stone Finish Throughout

Built solid, of one of the world's most prized building materials, Indiana Bedford limestone, with interior finish in St. Meinrad Indiana sandstone, the Church of St. Paul is adorned throughout with Dakota Sioux Indian design and symbolism. The edifice looms at the end of a Section Road ten miles south of the once busy Ravinia train depot. There the Chicago, Milwaukee & St. Paul Railroad steamed westward toward its terminus in the town of Platte. From Ravinia, every piece of construction material had to be trucked the ten miles to the building site—every stone, brick, bag of cement, bolt, tile, steel, window and door lumber—plus food for the workers. This weighed heavily on the surrounding school complex, which in the early1940s boarded 80 summer orphans and up to 450 students nine months of the year, with every need supplied, including transportation to their homes on 13 outlying reservations.

To be exact, not every building material came via rail. The most basic element was to be borne up from the prairie itself, by the enthusiastic hands of the school children. To ride the old flatbed trucks miles out onto the fields surrounding Marty, the boys jostled for position. Nearby homesteaders, brought close to the Reservation by the Land Sale of 1892, viewed as good riddance the piles of field stones cleared off their farms. But the stones would face much cracking by hand with sledge-hammers, and crushing in a rebuilt rock crusher before their final resting place in the concrete pours on the church, from the foundations and the main slabs to the soaring arches overhead.

This building source, product of nature—precious boulders from the carving out of the Great Central Plains—depended on the innate skills of the school children. These skills were already honed on several buildings in the past, riding the trucks to new exciting encounters with rabbits, snakes, prairie dogs and skunks. The rocks proved a fitting gift from venerable Mother Earth who sustains the human body in life and receives it in death.

A Brief Look at Events Leading Up to Marty

The Sioux knew the French fur traders with their black-robed Jesuit missionaries who plied the rivers of the Great Lakes region. They also dealt with the Spanish who maintained trading posts on the swift Missouri. Then followed years of isolation, when the Yanktons as well as a surprising number of other tribes, pressed hard for a Blackrobe of their own. The demands, including official letters and long, arduous trips by delegations, extended from 1641 to 1921.

The Treaty of 1858 moved the Yankton Sioux people 70 miles west to this Reservation from their wide buffalo range and their home at what is now the city of Yankton. As seen earlier, the Chiefs took action in 1866. Their persistence eventually led to the founding of St. Paul's Mission on the Reservation ten miles south of Ravinia, with a Post Office opened September 27, 1922, named Marty. The name honors Abbot Martin Marty, O.S.B., later Bishop of Dakota Territory, who in 1876 personally answered the Indians' pleas and committed his monastery St. Meinrad, Indiana, to help the Dakota tribes.

The Dream That Died in 1879

Shortly thereafter, in 1879, a heartbreaking attempt failed the Yanktons. With the help of Father J. F. Malo from Fort Randall across the Missouri River, the Cournoyers, Vandals and Picottes built St. Ann's School at Whetstone 30 miles upriver from the present Marty. The rough chalkrock building crumbled after the winter's freeze, and the three intrepid Sisters of the Presentation from Ireland eventually settled in Fargo, North Dakota. Years later it was to view these ruins that Father Sylvester often took new teachers on a drive past old St. Ann's. He lived under the somber reminder that his own valiant effort at Marty might fail.

Marty's First Tiny Chapel

Another effort came in 1913 with the help of Jesuit Father Henry Westropp from distant Pine Ridge across the Missouri River. He obtained the first Catholic house of worship exclusively for the Yanktons, dedicated by Bishop Thomas O'Gorman of Sioux Falls on October 22 that year as St. Paul's Mission Chapel. A carpenter from Wagner, Paul Einkopf and his crew built it with a $1,100 legacy from Mrs. Ellen Haggerty, a New York City seamstress. The Catholic Indian Bureau in Washington, D.C., paid $450 to Eugene Shooting Hawk (Brunot) for the land.

The beloved Father Westropp served on the mission circuit to St. Paul's until March of 1916, with a year of that time living in the tiny sacristy. This frame building, after many transformations, still serves at Marty in 2008.

THE "NEW" 1918 CHURCH (left) with ST. PAUL'S 1913 CHAPEL (right)—Between them is Father Sylvester's 1917 Model T Ford, stranded for the winter of 1919-1920 —EFC

Moving The 1918 Church

The narrow sacristy behind the first small chapel served as the only meeting place for the people. The leaders then looked around. In Wagner, 13 miles away, they found an old frame church building outgrown by St. John's Parish. They purchased it for $700. Then, undaunted, they set out to drag the structure across the rough prairie behind three big steam thrasher engines. They used a seeming miraculous catch from the Missouri River— huge timbers and heavy railroad chains that floated 150 miles downriver from the Chamberlain bridge washout. The move stretched into an ordeal of many months.

During the haul, the Spanish Influenza Pandemic raging in 1918 took the life of two workers: chief engineer Ishmael on November 1; and Jacob Red Horse, on December 3rd. Jacob was 18 years old. [The entire saga is detailed in *Blackrobe for the Yankton Sioux*, by this author.]

LABORIOUS HAUL ACROSS THE OPEN PRAIRIE: Marty's "new" 1918 church dragged behind three borrowed steam engines. The building was hauled 13 miles from Wagner starting in 1918 and not ready for use until 1922.

OSOTEWIN, SMOKE WOMAN, OR UNCI (GRANDMA) MARY WHITE TALLOW, here with her pipe, on a daily visit to her husband's grave in the old cemetery at Marty (moved in 1926). She lived to be 100. Photo by Cecilia Hettich, March, 1924.--EFC

Dollar Bills and Quilts

The school grew almost wholly from dollar bills, the sacrifice of benefactors around the U. S. They heard Father Sylvester's pleas, and grew to know and care for the Dakota Indians by reading his monthly newssheet called *The Little Bronzed Angel*.

Also, from earliest days, the women of Marty, led by venerable Grandma White Tallow, created rare porcupine quill and beadwork items. They quilted hundreds of vibrant colored Star Quilts for sale and raffle among benefactors in the east. The star design, lost in legend, represents eternal life, and is still today placed on the altar at Mass and in the casket of loved ones.

INTERIOR OF MARTY'S 1918 CHURCH, with the Four Evangelists on the ceiling; in use from 1921 to 1941--EFC

Thunder Horse, Zephier and Yellow Bird on the 1921 Pursuit

The three elders finally saw their hopes realized, in the person of Father Sylvester Eisenman from the St. Meinrad Benedictine Abbey in Indiana. The three journeyed a thousand miles to the Abbey and convinced Abbot Athanasius to appoint their itinerant missionary, Father Sylvester, as a permanent pastor. He was destined to work his entire 32 years of priesthood with the Dakota Indians: two years at Devils Lake and Fort Totten in North Dakota, where he learned the Dakota Sioux language, then exchanging places with Father Ambrose Mattingly, O.S.B., on a ten-mission trail out of Stephan,

YANKTON SIOUX ELDERS *at St. Meinrad Abbey, Indiana, after 1,000-mile journey, petitioning for a missionary of their own. Left to right, standing: Edward Yellow Bird and David Zephier (Black Spotted Horse); seated, Chief Thunder Horse.*

South Dakota, from 1918 to 1921. This grueling circuit included St. Paul's Mission (later named Marty) ten miles south of Ravinia, South Dakota. Father Sylvester served this Mission until his death, September 14, 1948.

Father Joseph Steiger lent lifelong aid to Father Sylvester after their seminary days together in Indiana. It was in his Earling, Iowa, parish in 1928 that a noted Exorcism took place. Described in booklet, *Begone Satan!,* of that year.

[Still another sponsor from Iowa, the state of the finest corn, was the "Popcorn Benefactor." He kept the children supplied with that aromatic treat on long tedious shut-in winter days.]

SEE NEXT PAGE ➜

The 'Backward Lists' Story

Yankton elder Grace Picotte remembers the lists: "Father Steiger from Iowa always brought a wooden bucket of candy for the school children. These buckets filled with envelopes Father Sylvester would bring to our homes Charles and Grace LaPointe Picotte and Ellis and Grace Johnson Zephier [later married to Joe Cournoyer] to address. We worked by lamplight from telephone books Father Sylvester had collected and Grandma Eisenman marked. Charlie called them 'backward lists.'"

These thin telephone directories from thousands of little towns were as precious as gold to Father Sylvester: begged from benefactors, and then marked by his mother, Elizabeth Hulsman Eisenman— names that suggested a background of faith and compassion. [The Indians named Grandma Eisenman Wahampi wastewin, Good soup woman.]

Elizabeth came in 1922 as "Mother Eisenman" but became "Grandma Eisenman" in 1929 when Leonard's family moved west to help.

ST. PAUL'S IN 1922, WITH HOME DESIGNED BY ST. KATHARINE DREXEL—*Viewed from northeast: L to R, newly built Sears & Roebuck rectory; the church hauled from Wagner in 1918; original 1913 chapel used as day school; two-story building at rear designed in 1922 by Mother (Saint) Katharine Drexel for first three teachers from her order in Philadelphia: Mother Liguori, Sister Hilda and Sister Ambrose.---EFC*

SAINT DEVOTED TO AMERICAN INDIANS AND BLACKS —
*Early benefactor of the Yankton Sioux, St. Katharine Drexel brought
steady insight and encouragement to Marty. On her many strenuous
trips she and her companion nun were often picked up in Sioux
City, Iowa, 135 miles east, to avoid changes in two more railroad
depots. This author often accompanied Josephine Eisenman, my
mother, on these trips; close-up memory of the starch in Mother
Katharine's wide linen coif.—Photo, SMOKE SIGNAL, St. Paul High
School 1941 Annual.*

A Brother-helper Comes

Beginning in 1922 with a full-day school session, Marty soon
found itself in a day-to-day struggle with an expanding boarding
school. The missionary's burden lightened in 1929, however, when
his brother Leonard John Eisenman and family moved west from
Indiana to help build and maintain the complex at Marty. We are
fortunate to have detailed, though infrequent, letters from Father
Sylvester and Leonard to their two priest-brothers Omer and
Edward, serving in Indiana Parishes. These rare documents picture
the mounting strain to keep pace with the ever increasing number
of parents seeking space for their children. The letters tell, especially,
the inside story of building the church.

1939— A Typical Year At Marty, Biding Time For A New Church

The urgency for a larger, fireproof church grew with each day, but other daily needs pressed on. The year 1939 was an example:

By 1939, Charles Mix County among eight in South Dakota, had just emerged from emergency drought designation the past autumn under Secretary of Agriculture Henry A. Wallace. Marty was a buzzing complex of self-contained school plant, with a purebred Holstein dairy farm, a Hereford beef herd, with garden and feed crops planted each year, amid recurring disappointments in the drought-grasshopper-dustbowl 1930s. Those were times when bad roads and lack of transportation made boarding schools the only answer. Up to 450 students, some from orphan nursery to high school diploma, were given food, shelter, recreation, medical, spiritual guidance and transportation, without any Government assistance. [Finally in 1933 the Government provided school bus rides instead of the "two-decker" truck rides, from outlying reservations, some as long as 500 miles.] Formerly, the tiniest children had scrambled onto the truck upper deck and bedded down on old soft worn clean coats for warmth. On one trip five stowaways managed to out-fox a busy truck driver.

EARLY DAYS. TRANSPORTING THE CHILDREN from North Dakota in the Mission truck to Marty in the 1920s. When the North Dakota school burned down, Marty accepted students from there, and later from other tribes.

As enrollment climbed, available resources shrank. The steady pursuit shows in Leonard's note April 16, 1939, to his brother in Indiana: "I picked up a cheap 1932 short wheelbase International truck in Sioux City [Iowa] last week and adapted an old steel dump bed to it for our farm. Farm work is coming along on time, the wheat being already out of the ground and much of the oats and barley sown.

Leonard added, "Very short of subsoil moisture. In spite of this, Fr. Syl transplanted several hundred Chinese elms heeled-in south of the shops, to Greenwood (school) and the Mission farm. He sure has the faith!" [This allusion to the constant determined tree-planting through the years explains the welcoming canopy of greenery that Marty enjoys in 2008. His brother Omer said of Father Sylvester, "Trees were the poetry of his life."]

PLANTING TREES—*Father Sylvester and willing workers, in thousands of plantings on the treeless plain, envisioned shade and shelter for posterity.*

LOOKING NORTH, TO BRUNO HOME *at right*

A QUICK LOOK at a typical work year at Marty shows what
an enormous extra load the few employees would shoulder in
building a church at this time. But postponement would only
increase the burden. The year 1939 is an example.

Skipping the New Year's Eve Party

New Year's Eve always found the employees of Marty celebrating
with a chili supper. All stayed up late for this best-of-the-year
event. Missing, however, were Father Sylvester and Leonard. The
two huddled in the waning hours over their annual review of jobs
completed. Here is their 1939 list:

1939 FINISHED WORK

Bought and delivered 81 head of Western
Hereford cows and one bull. *(See Appendixes Nos. 2
and 3 on the vital Farms, pages 80 and 82)*

Bought and delivered 101 head of western sheep
[experiment failed].

Built Community Building and new Rectory
complete (including fabrication of all bar
joists, columns, beams, windows, door frames,
cast stone, steel stairways, balcony railing,
marble base, stall partitions and screens—
weather-strip by others).

Built steam conduit (reinforced) from old line
to new Rectory.

Made heavy fill at new Rectory and playground
north of Bell Tower, and sod around Rectory.

Added small dwelling at West Farm.

Added to Peter Delorme's residence [employee,
Marty graduate].

Bought furniture for Community Building and
Rectory.

Relocated dish washing equipment in main kitchen. Welded together two copper Hobart dishwashers.

Bought $200 in band instruments.

Remodeled parapet wall and relocated Cross on Convent.

Built three food carts for Marty dining room.

Installed V-belt drive on air compressor.

Rebuilt motor on 1933 farm Chevrolet Pickup.

Bought roller skates and gym suits.

Traded 1936 Pickup for new 1940 Ford ¾ ton Pickup.

Built sand screening machine, and overhauled plaster mixer.

Completely rebuilt Caterpillar Diesel 70 (bought in 1938).

Traded 1936 IHC truck for 1939 IHC.

Mounted a Lincoln Welder (bought in 1938).

Finished brick cottage (mechanic Arnie Gau's) consisting of all wood trim, kitchen cabinet, varnish, sidewalks.

Built cabinets for High School Domestic Science, Chemistry cabinet, installed refrigerator and Skelgas equipment.

Installed improved control valve equipment on ammonia plant, and improved piping.

Replaced entire main sewer line on west side of Mission with 8" and 6", and installed manholes.

Installed glass rack and screen wire racks in stockroom.

Built drawing tables and drawing boards for shop classroom. [Leonard taught machine shop classes also.]

Painted interior of elevated water tank.

Built oak cabinets - Oblate Sisters.

Built three dining tables - Sisters of Blessed Sacrament.

Put up new cooling tower.

Installed guards on shop machinery.

Bought Router machine.

Bought lot and poured foundation only for St. Catherine's Chapel [outlying].

Rewired Grocery store.

Wired Bell Tower, St. Joseph's outer lights, and St. Katherine to street light system.

Replaced floor in old mess kitchen.

Moved slaughter house to West Farm.

Installed ventilator in roof on West Farm barn.

Bought roller skates and gym suits.

Poured 7 ft. sidewalk across north end of Mission, also walks at new Rectory and .

Replaced exterior breeching to smoke stack.

Added one toilet in Frame school, rebuilt shelving.

Installed flat wood rods in 4 1/2" Mission well

```
with new 3" line and screen.

Built steel slide for children at St. Placid
[baby] Home.

Installed V-belt drive on 6" farm well,
centrifugal pressure pump, and control of
distribution system.

Installed beams and columns in seed house,
farm, to carry additional weight.
```

Foremost Task, Gathering the School Children

About the "steady rush getting ready for the school year," Father Sylvester wrote his brother Omer on September 11, 1940:

"Delahoyde [seminarian] and I went to Standing Rock Reservation in North Dakota, and then on to Fort Berthold. We have a nice group of children from both those reservations. I accompanied the bus to Kansas last week, and we now have 52 Potawatomi boys and girls at Marty. They are exceptionally fine children. The next day we went to Wakpala, then to Cheyenne, and brought back 34 from those districts. In the meantime, the Winnebagos, Poncas, and Santees came in from Nebraska. Our enrollment now is 360, but we expect about 25 more within the next few days."

> Another part of Saint Katharine Drexel's legacy is her wholehearted assistance to Father Sylvester in founding a unique religious order in 1935, the Oblate Sisters of the Blessed Sacrament for American Indian women [in 1953 opened to non-Indian women]. See later mention and photos of the Oblates for their multifaceted, ongoing work at the Mission.

Loving Presence of Saint Katharine Drexel's Nuns

Climbing numbers at St. Paul's School in 1940 indicated its excellent reputation, one built through 18 years of hard work and devotion of Mother (later Saint) Katharine Drexel's order, Sisters of the Blessed Sacrament. At the order's motherhouse near Philadelphia in 1922 Father Sylvester had pled for teachers, and waited until Mother Katharine adjusted schedules and assigned to Marty three of the many who volunteered. Without these devoted missionary women, Marty would not have developed.

SISTERS OF THE BLESSED SACRAMENT AT MARTY IN 1941—For 60 years, from September 5, 1922, the first night spent in South Dakota listening to the clatter of the windmill, the Sisters of Mother (Saint) Katharine Drexel's order taught and cared for the children at Marty. Their story is told in 8TH LANDING: THE YANKTON SIOUX MEET LEWIS AND CLARK, by this author. Shown here, in January, 1941, are L to R; back row: Sr. Chabanel, Sr. Gerardine, Sr. Aloysia, Sr. Theophane, Sr. Celeste, Sr. Cecily; middle row: Sr. Anastasia, Sr. Henrietta, Sr. Louis, Sr. Sylvester, Sr. Agnese, Sr. Benedict Joseph; front row: Sr. Florence, Sr. Bonifacius, Sr. Margaret Mary, Sr. M. Liguori, Sr. Joachim, Sr. Edward and Sr. Ambrose.

The 1940 Building Decision

By 1940, plans for a permanent church at Marty were developing in Father Sylvester's mind. The old decaying frame structure, enlarged and patched many times, was no longer adequate. He toured reservations and studied Indian art for ideas.

At home, he assembled the planners (Sisters and other leaders). They squeezed down onto benches in a sea of dining tables, the only surface broad enough to unroll the blueprints and to plan. This in an echoing cavern that within a few hours would fill with clatter of dishes and chatter of hungry youngsters.

Grade school children in the art class of Sister Theophane [Sister of the Blessed Sacrament] produced beadwork designs for decorating the ceiling beams and other facets of the new church. Stained glass artists snapped photos of different generations on the Reservation for their models.

Oblate Sisters Christine Hudson and Madeleine LeCompte brought Indian designs to Father Sylvester. His long-held wish to revive the dying art of beadwork among the children was only one of numerous contributions made by the Oblate Sisters [seen later].

On a two-week trip to study California and Southwest missions, Father Sylvester took with him his brother Leonard. Since 1929, building after building went up to meet the expanding demand. And Leonard's wife Josephine and their four children [another, Joseph, born later in South Dakota] adjusted to life on the reservation, from their Southern Indiana home of Loogootee.

All but two of the eleven fireproof buildings at Marty received Leonard's direction and detail. Trained at Winona Technical Institute in Indianapolis, he had been caught in the mechanical hysteria of the newly discovered automobile. He labored on Henry Ford's Indianapolis assembly line in1914— pure jubilation the day Ford raised a day's pay to $5.00. But at the same time Ford sped up the belts beyond the strength of many workers to endure. Leonard then pioneered in Southern Indiana with a garage and dealership for Hudson & Essex, among others.

LEONARD EISENMAN'S OFFICE— Now at Marty, with his shelves of engineering books beside his desk, after eleven years putting up buildings at Marty, and many learning trips to distant plants, Leonard was, in 1940, ready to face the challenge of a lifetime. He would erect the crowning jewel at the heart and center of the mission at Marty. It was a staggering test of Providence. There were no bids. No contractor. No companies with heavy equipment, forms, scaffolding, lifts, cranes. No

skilled sub-contractors within miles. But Marty had on site the genius of two overseers, brothers, who would put heart and soul into this act of faith together with the Yankton Sioux people.
—Photo from 1941 High School Annual, SMOKE SIGNAL.

This writer had the privilege of working in the business and construction office of her Dad, Leonard, at Marty from mid-1936 to mid-1938. One way to find him was to ride the open construction elevator on the high school building site in the whipping wind, with a clipboard of checks and letters to be signed before Matt McCarthy picked up the mail for the Ravinia depot ten miles away. . . .Another extreme was reaching through the thick brick furnace wall with a glass of cold milk to Leonard welding in the searing interior, while the whole Mission shivered in overcoats. . . . The day-laborers received cash in their pay envelopes, which this author took up to St. Benedict's Building second floor for filling. At times the office had to wait for the daily incoming mailbag to yield enough dollars.

The church, Father Sylvester said, was to use all new material, not second-hand recycled material, as in all previous buildings, for it was to be <u>a place of worship worthy of the Indians' long enduring faith and sacrifice</u> .

THE MACHINE SHOP HUMMED *with action below the Men Employees' Building and St. Katherine's Building to the north. In the narrow space between was Leonard's business office. At left is the 1937 Ford 1½ ton truck.—EFC*

Despite this "all-new" specification on the materials, the tools of construction at hand remained primitive. In all the years past, only recycled, second-hand tools, under the hand of inventive genius, served the purpose. Trucks groaning from the unceasing hauls overwhelmed the shop for repairs. The main machine shop was already crowded with ironwork for the church.

THE HIGH SCHOOL JOB had intervened, leaving the shop space only recently cleared of hundreds of forms for stone-making. These precise stones decorated the high school building, completed September 11, 1938, amazingly, less than six months after excavation began (March 22, the day the ice broke up on the Missouri). State accreditation had come earlier to St. Paul's High on October 16, 1936, with a curriculum stronger than closest towns Wagner, Lake Andes or Ravinia [later torn down]. Marty offered science; the others did not. Where in the entire realm could one find a high school finished in elegant marble wainscoting and partitions, with solid oak doors and trim, and steel staircase? All these saved from a venerable six-story bank building that once stood on the corner of 5th and Jackson in Sioux City, Iowa, 135 miles east. Razing and moving a six-story masonry building across town is a feat, but hauling its salvage <u>135 miles</u> is another. The Mission built a special trailer to handle

50-foot beams, traveling by night to avoid traffic holdups. The bank building accounted for the vintage hardwood floor and trim in the 1935 gymnasium, as well as for the high school.

Early in 1940 Leonard made three trips to Omaha, looking for ideas on keeping the overworked school kitchen, bakery and laundry running. "I stopped for an hour at Father Flanagan's Boys' Town," he wrote, with a hint of envy, " to see his new kitchen and dining hall. It is the <u>last word.</u> He is sure putting on a building boom. Three new dormitories just finished."

More Power to the Snowplow

Snow time rolled around, and the snowplow needed more power. Leonard wrote his brother in Indiana November 19, 1940: "Father Syl finally agreed to have us fit the 1936 plow from the old Holt tractor to the Diesel. A big job. In order to get a piece of seven-inch I-beam to extend the side rails of the snow plow, I had to get a crew of 30 kids and shovel through a five-foot drift that filled the entire yard west and south of the machine shed [at the farm]. Luckily, I remembered pretty well the layout of the steel and found it in about an hour."

LIFE EMERGENCY—Plowing through 13 miles to Dr. Thomas Duggan's Hospital above Buche's Dry Goods Store in Wagner. Marty's mechanic and basketball coach Arnie Gau and wife Eva followed behind the "Cat" in time for the birth of their first daughter Rita in early 1936.---EFC

First a Demolition

OLD CHURCH REDUCED TO LUMBER — *The glorious adventure of erecting the church faced one big obstacle. The old frame structure had to be torn down. The high school boys still remember the start March 5, 1941, ripping it apart board-by-board with crowbars;*

every nail pulled. Boards were stacked according to size to form up the concrete on the new church. The buckets of old nails waited to reinforce the concrete as each wheelbarrow dumped into the forms. All this, after the big move of entire interior furnishings to a place in the gymnasium, where daily worship could continue. Frame dwellings either side were to be moved later.

Ready to Dig the Basement

Time for digging the basement came. That would mean a contractor with a big backhoe and front-end loader, but Marty had neither. Leonard outfitted the Diesel with the two-yard Fresno, to scrape out the sand. The high sand content led him to double the strength of foundation specifications set by Cincinnati architect Paul Schulte.

No Contractor's Shack

Marty had no contractor's shack. However, only a few feet from the gaping foundation sat the old Sears & Roebuck rectory with a handy back-room door newly-cut to open onto the site—but robbing Grandma Eisenman of her room. From 1922 this small bungalow had served as priest's home, main office, used clothing dispensary, and soup kitchen for hungry families on the Reservation, until replaced by a fireproof residence in 1939. [After finishing the church, the Marty crew had to move this old landmark rectory onto a new foundation to the west, nearer the creek.]

Back To The Rock Piles

Countless trips out onto the prairie with the flatbed truck raised columns of dust, to bring in the stones for the big "pours." Peter

EVERYBODY HELPS AT THE ROCK PILE.

AT THE SAND PIT---- High school boys vying for fastest loads.-- *EFC*

Delorme was one of many truck drivers. Next came the cracking. Rocks bigger than 12 inches called for the sledge-hammer crew. Father Sylvester, an old hand with the sledge, showed the trick of finding the telltale seam on which to make the blow. Father Benno Fellinger with his long arms was an expert, also. Father Sylvester welcomed the summer help, seminarians from the east, and the chance for them to "toughen up" on the rock pile. In 1941 they were Benno Fellinger, Stanislaus Maudlin, Louis Delahoyde and Joseph Dieckhaus. Daylight lingered far into the summer evenings, a backdrop for the tympanum from the sledge pile, the long arms in rhythm, straining to build a house for God. [The seminarians later served as priests on the Dakota missions.] *For a parallel note in history see Appendix No. 4. page 82.*

Willing Workers

April 26, *Little Bronzed Angel:* The boys go out on the truck today, gathering stones from far and wide on the prairie. Another crew hauls sand for the concrete. And still another helps with the steel reinforcing rods that go into the forms.

SUNDAY CROWD EXPLORES THE BUSTER

ROCK BUSTING IN 100-DEGREE HEAT — *The satisfying sound of progress was recorded by Father Sylvester on July 9, 1941: "The thermometer reads close to 100. Our windows are open wide on the shady side. From 50 yards away comes the crushing thud of the rock buster. It is a new home-made contraption in which a heavy weight falls from a height of 20 feet upon a mighty rock, splitting it in two or three parts, preparing it for the rock crusher. The boys of last year would envy the ability of this big rock buster. With one mighty wallop it does to a rock what a boy could do in half an hour. The ground around Marty shakes when this buster goes a bustin." [True words.]*

HOME-MADE ROCK CRUSHER *—Operating on a Hupmobile engine, first it crushed, then screened to size. The high school boys picked the rocks under 12 inches to feed into it until the crankshaft broke. But Pete Thomas was ready on the lathe to make a new one of steel.*

First Wall Section Goes Up

On May 2, 1941, *The Little Bronzed Angel* announced:

"The first section of the concrete wall of the new church is completed today. All day long, until an hour after dark, the wheelbarrows of concrete find their way to the wooden forms the

carpenters have built. The schoolboys work in relays so they won't get too tired. Others are busy dropping stones into the soft concrete.

The kitchen, too is doing overtime today. The girls appear at 9:30 and again at 4 o'clock with baskets of sandwiches for our faithful workers. It is the First Friday of the month, and the boys, of their own accord, arise at 5 o'clock to attend Mass and receive Holy

Communion. At 9:30 P.M. the work is completed. Another supply of sandwiches shows up and everyone is happy. Ten minutes later the doorbell at the rectory rings. Father Sylvester is surprised to see a large crowd of Indian boys standing outside, "Father, can we sleep long tomorrow?" Permission readily granted.

> **A torrent of rain threatened the newly poured basement slab late in the night of June 20, 1941. Leonard rushed out to check the damage. His toe caught in the metal mud-scraper mat and jerked out the nail.**

Arms Reaching Out

The concentrated effort on the church did not stop Father Sylvester from helping out another missionary. On June 23 he drove Ed Schulte, his Cincinnati architect, to Garrison, North Dakota, to assist the Sisters of that Motherhouse with their building project. Years earlier, Marty came to the aid of St. Ann's in Belcourt, North Dakota, and St. Joseph's in Chamberlain, South Dakota.

SCAFFOLDING

FEEDING THE CONCRETE MIXER ---*It held one cubic yard at a time, needing three or four bags of cement, plus enough crushed rock or sand as the day's pour required.*

Cool Water on the Job

Father Sylvester and Leonard were concerned about their brother, Father Edward Eisenman, hospitalized in Vincennes, Indiana, with a heart attack. The only time for Leonard to write was before the seven o'clock whistle blew for work. The July 24th thermometer read 114 in the shade. Leonard's July 31st letter opened: "Father Syl surprised us by arriving home after supper last evening. I was working in the shop till 10 P. M. So hot yesterday the men had to buy dozens of bottles of pop to keep up their spirits, so I decided to make up a cooler for water. We finished it except for testing and hooking up to the water line and sewer. It is a copper coil in a double container with cork insulation, cover and fountain. Will use ice from the ice plant and operate on pressure. It will save a lot of time and make the men feel good. There are 400 enrolled in the school, and 15 more expected." [Someone proofing this text queried this author: "Did Leonard ever patent any of his inventions?"!!]

Five days later, August 5th, the cooler stood its ground against the stifling heat. With steel all in place for the main slab, 750 sacks of cement fed the mixer in another grueling "pour." The mission newssheet *Little Bronzed Angel* informed the benefactors: "Father Sylvester says Mass at 3:15 A.M., after which the work starts. All day long the wheelbarrows are filled and emptied. At 10 P.M. the job is finished. Tomorrow will be a free day for our workmen."

18-HOUR POUR

THE CORNERSTONE- LAYING —*A shutterbug stepping through rebars in the foundation, with his Kodak Brownie Box Camera, ready to photograph Leonard Eisenman setting the cornerstone May 25, 1941. It was the Silver Jubilee of Father Sylvester's ordination as a priest.---EFC*

INTERIOR COLUMNS GOING UP

Tragedy at Pearl Harbor

The Japanese attacked the U. S. Navy at Hawaii December 7, 1941, when the church was half finished. Then began a frantic scramble for supplies and workmen. Even before the United States declared war on Japan, the Mission could not compete in the wage market. Yet the timetable for construction is amazing to read. On March 5, 1941, the old frame church was vacated, the structure dismantled <u>in one week.</u> The first concrete pour was April 5. By May 14, carpenters were impossible to find: The U. S. Government had picked a crucial time to siphon off workers. Its colossal Fort Randall Dam project just a few miles northwest paid high wages.

Faithful Workmen

Workman Bill Hoffman fell January 23, 1942, from a scaffold. Though Vic Campbell caught him, the injuries plagued Bill for a long time. Unable to do heavy work, Bill could drive teachers

and others from the Mission to medical help in Wagner, Mitchell, Yankton, even to Sioux City, Iowa. John Doty stayed on as a foreman until the end. Other old standbys, Ab Vinatieri of Yankton finished the plumbing; Ralph Tessier of Mitchell did the roofing; Matt Thome the plastering; and electricians Leonard "Shorty" Battin and Frank Kohoutek of Yankton stuck to the job. Stonemasons from Yankton, Gus and Henry Morgen, veterans of other Marty buildings, laid the last stone August 20, 1942, to the ringing of bells.

World War II virtually wiped out the labor supply. The burden increased as many longtime employees left for better paying jobs in the war effort. John Doty, however, stayed on until May. Grandma Eisenman wrote of him: "He was labor foreman on high school, community building, rectory and church, so they gave him a little blowout when he left. It was nice for John to stick with us through this work. So many go after the defense jobs."

No list of local workmen is available, but this author remembers several: Josiah Franklin, Mose Hart, Adam Iron Hawk, Lellwyn

Selwyn, Victor and Pat Campbell, Joe Picotte, Ellis and Edward Zephier, Charles Mallory, George Drapeau, Cecil Provost, Hank Selwyn, Hank Hare; Clarence Packard, Peter Delorme, Raymond and Romeo Dauphinais, Steven Cournoyer, Edward Roman, Arnie Gau, Joseph Cranford, Ramsey Bartlett, Chris Broderson, Logan Wood, and Ray Flying Hawk. Memories of the latter:

> This author was in the back seat of our family Ford next to Ray Flying Hawk as my mother, Josephine, drove full speed 13 miles to Wagner. Ray was covered in sweat from the hot, dusty harvest field. Nurse Mary Jane Borden, alongside, was sucking the poison from a rattlesnake bite in his arm. We had to shift places quickly, as the west wind blew the blood back into the car when Mary Jane spat it out the window. Mary Jane, from Rushville, Indiana, had volunteered when the Reservation was without doctor or nurse. [Finally a doctor came to another part of the Reservation, but he had no telephone.] —For more on automobiles at Marty, see Appendix No. 5, page 82.

AB VINATIERI, THE PLUMBER, came out from Yankton City with his big black dog Sprinkler, and bunked at the Mission during several building stints. [Literally bunked, as Grandma Eisenman, with her old Minnesota treadle machine, sewed the sheets for the workmen from bolts of muslin— and then kept them laundered.] One day Ab hurried to the small Post Office on the second floor of St. Benedict's Hall. Behind the grill was Mary Becking, efficient postal clerk who was to serve almost four decades. She also dispensed replacement light bulbs. Ab forgot to bring in the old one, and was refused a new one. At that, he nominated Mary Becking for County Constable. The charged air around Marty remained high for some time.

Trim Material Arriving

"Quite a few of the tiles are now on the roof," Leonard noted on February 8, 1942, "& the copper work going along with it. We received the aluminum grille work for around the belfry. The bronze thresholds & stair tread for important locations also are here & we have promise of bronze hardware."

POURING TWO MORE ARCHES FOR THE CHURCH —By
November 14, 1941, Father Sylvester announced: "Two more
concrete arches for the church are poured. Every few hours the
crowd of boys shifts, between school work and concrete work. At
intervals a cheer goes up as the girls appear on the scene with more
sandwiches. <u>*Never too tired, the boys open their basketball season*</u>
<u>*tonight with a win."*</u>

Final, Massive Arch Out of Danger

The final and largest arch, Leonard wrote Aug. 16, 1942, "is now being built and is out of the "danger" stage. There was a course of stone to lay on a single arch form clear across the area, the width of the stones being 3 ½ ft. and thickness 4 inches. The form was only two 2x8's bolted together with angles for splices. The short angles were tack-welded to the iron pipe posts of the scaffold for support. As the stones came closer and closer to the keystone position, I couldn't leave the job anymore. I kept my hand on the last stones laid, as one could rock the whole business without effort! The keystone brought a lot of relief, but I felt better yet when they completed the first 8 feet of brickwork over the stones. Then they filled the space under the concrete arch at the bottom with brick which prevents a buckle. So now, with two days to set, she is as safe as in Abraham's bosom. Still have to set two angle iron forms for the molding stones on each side of the arch.

> **"Must plaster the high wall behind altar before we can take down the elevator. Took some Sisters up on it yesterday but they were stranded up in the scaffold for a quarter of an hour while I went to find some fuses to replace those I burnt out. They were working on St. Christopher before I returned."**—About Leonard's missing violin fingers see Appendix No. 6, page 82.

All Hands Want To Be a Part

Oblate Sister Christine added: "We Sisters joined in, sifted sand, hauled bricks and crushed rocks. We searched for the next number on the limestone blocks laid out in the field, for the stonemasons. Some of those stones were heavy load for four men."

Oblate Sister Anthony Davis, 65 years later, remembered how she and Sister Madeleine Le Compte searched for rocks the right size for

HIGH JINKS ON THE ELEVATOR— It was an exuberant time. To the dismay of their mother, on August 16 Father Sylvester and Leonard gave the teachers and cameras a precarious ride on the construction elevator before it was removed. Sister Christine Hudson, one of the Oblate Sisters of the Blessed Sacrament, recalled: "Grandma came by and scolded her sons for dropping us in jerks of the elevator for fun."

Home-made Steel Elevator Shaft, 1942

ELEVATOR SHAFT—On February 8, 1942, Leonard wrote: "A home-made steel elevator shaft now stands up on the first floor slab ready to lift the concrete into the forms for the pillars. We have speeded up the hoist 20% in order to be able to handle the 1,000 trips (two wheelbarrows each) in one day for the tower slab. Everyone will be played out when that pour is over. The school boys take half a day off to go swimming in the reservoir over by the farm after last night's good thumping rain. And the aluminum cross is on the way from Cincinnati."

ROOF FORMING UP

the crusher—to make gravel for the terrazzo floors.

Another, Sister Inez Jetty, recalled in 2007: "The church was already built when I came to high school at Marty. I didn't get to lift a stone. I gasped when I saw the magnificent mural [of heaven] behind the main altar."

FATHER SYLVESTER FOUNDED this order for American Indian Women in 1935. Mother (Saint) Katharine Drexel sent two Sisters of her order to train the initial candidates in religious life. Open to non-Indian members since 1953, these South Dakota nuns hold a prodigious record of service: in spiritual guidance, certified teaching, quantity cooking, Star Quilt making, beadwork, faith and funeral apostolate, food and clothing for the poor. They comfort the frail elderly in three outlying towns. The Oblate Sisters of the Blessed Sacrament attract women to work with all families in the ever evolving apostolate on the Reservation.

WORK GOES ON IN SNOW

Men and Boys Disappear

By September, 1942, forty of the high school boys had disappeared. Only 12 remained. Father Sylvester reported: "Some are in the service in all parts of the world, some in the harvest fields, or in war work. It is the first chance in their young lives to earn a worthwhile wage. Well they know their poor parents can use some of their earnings. Every household is short some needed article or piece of furniture, a new team or mower."

Marty graduate Abraham Little Beaver from Winnebago gave his life clearing a runway on the Island of New Guinea. Operating a giant Caterpillar earthmover with the CB's Construction Battalion, he was struck by falling trees.

COMPLETION DATE [the date set for consecration ceremonies] loomed only five weeks ahead, when Leonard's hurried

(Continued p. 49)

SANDSTONE BLOCKS READY FOR CHURCH INTERIOR— Looking toward High School to east.

READY FOR INTERIOR STONEWORK

SCULPTURE IN PLACE ABOVE ENTRANCE – ST. PAUL APOSTLE OF THE NATIONS

(Cntinued from page 46)

note to his brothers Omer and Ed in Indiana described progress
on the church. He managed to write every two or three months. By
November 8, 1942, the supply of workmen had shrunk to the lowest:

"We are barely able to hold onto enough common labor to
keep the church work going. The girls were a big help. The dirt and
construction debris is gradually disappearing from the bldg. and
premises. Using any skilled help we can borrow from the Public

RAILINGS & PEWS—*Every inch of space in the carpenter shop held
railings, doors, pews and other millwork, affording the high school boys
a unique exposure to that trade, and chance for good future jobs.*

Service Co. [of nearby towns]. Only one more ornamental iron
fixture for us to make now—the door to the Baptistery. It will weigh
over 800 pounds, using mostly 1-inch square steel bars, which we
happen to have in stock. Interior woodwork is the slowest thing."

Even the little girls begged to carry one brick.

Saga of the Doors

Eight heavy oak exterior doors emerged from the carpenter shop. Rows of brass medallions held each together. The rosettes, roughcast in a foundry miles away, arrived in kegs, like nail kegs. Lathes in the Marty shop burnished them, drilled and threaded them. The medallions remain a welcome sight to each visitor approaching the doors. Their historic fame was to resurface, as in the following story:

> For 55 years the medallions held—until May of <u>1996</u>, when nostalgia for the old high school days at Marty moved a small band of graduates to return and restore the aging portals. The alumni would feel once again the satisfaction of clamping in place the dozens of brass medallions. Several in the group had become well-known building contractors. They found decades of weather and wear had left a mark. Now, two days of unusual rain at Marty kept the new finish from drying in the shop, but the

RESTORING THE DOORS —*A Wagner Post article May 22, 1996, noted the love and pride evinced in this nostalgic event with: "These guys have all done well in life and they got most of their education here at St. Paul's." Wearing their hats that say "Marty Restoration Project" are (L-R) Joe Eisenman, Joseph "Gus" LaFramboise, Leonard "L.J." Eisenman, Jr.; Sylvester "Smacks" LaFramboise and Clifford "Whitey" LaFramboise. They are shown with one of the doors they are refinishing at St. Paul's Church—Wagner Post photo by Carol Harrell, with permission.*

busy carpenters arranged for the job to be completed in Wagner, 13 miles away, and underwrote the cost. All at Marty shared the jubilation and feasting with those loyal alumni. Coming from Arizona, North and South Dakota, Idaho and Minnesota, they included those in the accompanying photo, plus Charles Belgarde, Francis and Steve Cournoyer. Joining them were Benedictine Fathers Daniel Madlon and Stan Maudlin, oldtimers formerly stationed at Marty. Afterwards, Sister Mary Francis Poitra, Oblate Sister of the Blessed Sacrament, wrote: "The doors are all very easy to lock now."

Time for the Big Bells in the Church Tower

Plans for the big bronze bells in the new church had faced a rocky start a year earlier. Copper was scarce. The U. S. began stockpiling war materials, and Stuckstede Company in St. Louis had barely enough copper and tin on hand for Marty's bells. Father Sylvester wrote his brother Omer September 19, 1941: "I was in Bloomington [Indiana] Monday about the stone [Indiana limestone for the

RINGING OF THE NEW BELLS —Superior of the Blessed Sacrament Sisters at Marty, Mother Liguori, posted in her diary October 8, 1941: "The new bells arrived and sounded for all to hear at supper time." The inscription on the large one is: Sanctissimo Patre Nostro Benedicto: Ausculta O Fili (Our most holy father Benedict: "Hear O Son." And on the smaller bell: "Sanctae Teresiae At Infanto Jesu (Saint Therese of the Infant Jesus): "I shall let roses fall upon the earth." [Words quoted from Saint Benedict and Saint Therese of Lisieux.]

exterior]. Then to St. Louis to contact Emil Frei, the art glass people, till 8 P.M. Next morning I called at the bell foundry and our two bells were already cast. Good thing we ordered early."

The Big Hoist

The day finally arrived. On April 20, 1942, Leonard's crew rigged a cable from a beam extending from the belfry out in mid air, to hoist the bells 110 feet up to the church tower. They used the truck to furnish power. All held their breath as the big bells went up. Then they dismantled the hoist tower.

GRANDMA WHITE TALLOW (left), and spry at age 99 (below, fourth from right) with Father Sylvester (far right).

LONGTIME EMPLOYEE ARNIE GAU RECALLED : "In all the ceremony of blessing the bells, Unci (Grandma) White Tallow insisted we let down one that was already hoisted half way up. It was her bell and she placed her hand on it in blessing and prayer before we pulled it up again. She wore her finest clothes for the occasion. There were Indian dances and a big feast outdoors."

BLESSING THE BELLS

Romance of the Bells

From the heights of joy to the depths of grief, bells carry us through life's moments. Ever since the Chinese 2,000 B. C., and the Benedictine monks in Italy in the 500s A.D., man has enjoyed the comforting peal from tower and parapet. The Mission Bells of the Southwest Padres; the Bells of St. Mary's in Bing Crosby's time; even the jingle bells of Christmas, hold memories. Early on, the Reservation leaders around Marty began a "bells fund." The lack of clocks made the hope of a ringing reminder very appealing.

First came the 1937 Bell Tower, attached to St. Joseph's Building. Grandma White Tallow paid for one of the four bells to hang in it. The tower was designed by Anton Joseph Barthuber (name later changed to Barth). Anton came as a teenager from Germany, with his zither and cuckoo clocks, driven by the Hitler threat. Also, he had heard about the great engineering feat, Boulder Dam , planned by President Herbert Hoover. Anton lived to be a world-renowned engineer in Chicago. But first he learned English at Marty, while leaving evidence of his cabinet- making skills in every corner of the mission and outlying chapels.

Later, the 1937 Bell Tower suffered demolition, but not the loss of memories attached to it. Poignant moments occurred every day in and around Marty. One such, at the blessing of the old Bell Tower, was a secret known only to Father Sylvester's family. The date October 13, 1937, marked the Golden Wedding Anniversary of his mother, Elizabeth Mary Hulsman Eisenman. Widowed for 42 years with four children, she had devoted her life to her three priest sons, wherever needed. [Beginning in 1922, Elizabeth spent 26 years helping at the Yankton Sioux mission.] For the bell blessing, her son Omer wrote a few personal lines. This author, then a teenager, found them so touching as to copy them in her own memory book:

"No doubt Papa [Edward Landelin Eisenman, Sr.] was looking down from heaven when those bells were blessed on your fiftieth wedding anniversary, and their ringing must have wakened memories in your heart. A long story, but a happy ending; weary years, but pealing bells on the home stretch. And those bells would not be ringing on the Dakota prairies if you had not kept them ringing in your heart during those long fifty years."

The Cross, The Pinnacle

The happiness of the moment shows in Father Sylvester's news:

PLACING THE CROSS
—Historic moment April 14, 1942, placing the cross and lightning rod atop the 167-foot steeple. L to R, Leonard Eisenman, Jr., 16; Father Sylvester Eisenman; Leonard Eisenman, Sr.

"At seven o'clock this evening, April 13, 1942, as the sun sinks on the western prairie, a long-awaited event takes place at Marty. Everyone gathers at the foot of the spire of the new church. It is now ready for the cross. We have all worked hard on the new church, and often we dreamed of the day when this cross would occupy the most prominent place at the Mission. We are sure the cross in the sky will raise the thoughts, motives and intentions of everyone

SCAFFOLD AT BELFRY LEVEL — *old belltower below at left*

here to the eternal Heaven that we are destined for. A benefactor in Michigan donated the cross when, on a recent visit he said, *'I can see where every dollar has been well spent."*

Raymond Dauphinais, Marty graduate and longtime mechanic, recalled:

"Father Sylvester and Leonard laid the capstone and lifted the cross 167 feet up in the wind. They positioned it according to direction signs from Louis Delahoyde perched above the high school on the east, and myself in the bell tower of St. Joseph's Building, southeast. The bells rang out."

THE CROSS, symbol of bitter suffering, echo of heartbreak in a race once corralled on reservations, yet nobly clinging to a deeper hope.

Ultimate Push to Finish

Added behind-the-scenes excitement shows in an interview with Marty's art teacher, Sister Theophane. This author visited her and other surviving Marty pioneers at the Motherhouse of the Sisters of the Blessed Sacrament in Cornwells Heights (later Bensalem) Pennsylvania, in June, 1975. Artistic finish on the church, Sister Theophane fondly recalled, rushed ahead until the final hours before the grand consecration ceremony of December 17, 1942:

"From my art class Father Sylvester took a sheaf of the students' Indian beadwork patterns to inspire the window and ceiling designs. The sheaf came back to me well thumbed. Traditional Indian colors were used: white, black, red, yellow, green for the earth; blue for the sky.

"People thought the Stations of the Cross were done by the same artists as the mural. But Cecilia Grinnell did them in the classroom. Father asked me to order the finest canvas, paint and brushes for them. There would be no inferior materials in the making of the church." [Cecilia was a high school senior from Elbowoods, North Dakota, in the art class of Sister Theophane.]

STAINED GLASS WINDOWS

"Emil Frei of St. Louis designed the 18 stained-glass windows. His father was a Bavarian glassmaker. The artists took snapshots of school children and adults around Marty as models."

—Sister Theophane.

Do This In
Remembrance
of Me.
(Last Supper)

What Wilt Thou
Have Me Do ?
(St. Paul)

Listen My
Son To The
Directions Of
Thy Instructor.
(St. Benedict)

Thou Art A
Priest Forever,
According To
The Order of
Melchisedech
(Priesthood)

FOUR of 18 WINDOWS. Photos from *A Celebration of Praise: Diamond Jubilee Oblate Sisters,* Marty, 1995.

Consecration Day Recorded

Newspapers around the state and nation recorded the event. Among them **THE LAKE ANDES WAVE** headlined:

MAGNIFICENT, NEW CATHOLIC CHURCH AT MARTY MISSION DEDICATED TODAY

The dedication ceremonies of the magnificent new church at Marty this Thursday afternoon marks a milestone in the life and achievement of Father Sylvester and his brother Leonard J. Eisenman who have devoted the past twenty years to the building of the Indian mission at Marty. The Most Reverend William Brady, Bishop of the Sioux Falls Diocese, will preside at the ceremonies, assisted by the Rt. Rev. Ignatius Esser, Abbot of St. Meinrad, Ind.; the Rt. Rev. Columban Thuis of New Orleans, La., and many other clergy and prelates from near and distant points.

The Rev. Leonard P. Sardo of Lake Andes will be one of the Thurifers or incense bearers. Several auto loads of friends from here will attend a part of the service. Extensive invitations have not been issued as the Marty parish of Indians are considered the first guests but interested friends are welcome.

Marty Mission, twenty years ago had its beginning with a few frame wind-swept buildings on the prairie, and on the same site there now raises a beautiful city devoted to the religion and education of the Indian race. Especially for the youth and its development into useful trained citizens. Thus has this dream been realized.

The fireproof dormitories to protect students and workers were built first, then brick school buildings and a large gymnasium; later, now, the crowning glory of all, an elaborate temple for the worship of God.

The work on this building was done by local labor under the direct supervision of the Mission, with John Doty of Ravinia acting as labor foreman. About twenty Indian and white men were employed regularly on the job. The upper floor of the Gymnasium was used as a church while the new one was in progress.

THE WAGNER POST in a December 17 article, reported:

> South Dakota and Charles Mix County salute Father
> Sylvester for building the finest Catholic Indian Mission in
> the U. S. A. at Marty.
>
> Twenty-four years ago a slim young priest came from the
> banks of the Wabash in Indiana to the prairies of Dakota
> to do missionary work among the Indians. Filled with
> enthusiasm and zeal like the builders of old he found the
> bleak prairies, and amid a few Indian shacks he started his
> mission. All through the years of drought, grasshoppers,
> and pestilence he worked. He brought his brother Leonard
> Eisenman, a master mechanic, here from Indiana and for
> 13 years he assisted, designed and helped build the finest
> group of buildings in the northwest to house the 400 Indian
> children who were obtaining their education here, being fed,
> clothed and educated on the charity of interested friends.
>
> The church and mission is a fitting monument to the great
> and good Indian Missionary, Father Sylvester. . . .The five-

OFFICIATING AT THE CEREMONY OF CONSECRATION are, L to R: Rev. Timothy Sexton, O.S.B.; Rev. Edward Eisenman, Bishop William O. Brady, Rev. Omer Eisenman, and Rev. Sylvester Eisenman, O.S.B., with acolytes Clement Zephier and one unidentified.—EFC.

hour dedication service, which began at 8:30 in the morning concluded with Pontifical High Mass.

[*The above two articles were reprinted in the January 15, 1943, bilingual Marty newspaper,* CATHOLIC INDIAN HERALD, or EYANPAHA.]

A week earlier on December 10th , the *WAGNER POST* announced:

The new church is unique in many respects. At most any point, one can easily see that it is an Indian Mission Church with portrayal of Indian design throughout. The large stone carving over the entrance depicts St. Paul, the Apostle of the Nations, and with him an Indian family. The beams and panels in the ceiling are decorated with authentic Indian design. The stained glass windows are distinctively Indian in character.

Sandstone from the quarries of St. Meinrad, Indiana, was used to line the major part of the interior. The framework is of reinforced concrete and brick. The

BISHOP WILLIAM O. BRADY and MR. A. B. VINATIERI SETTING THE ALTAR STONE.

DRESSING THE ALTAR AT CONSECRATION OF CHURCH—*The altar stands over the very spot where, at dusk 24 years earlier, a circle of moccasined men waited to welcome Father Sylvester for the first time.*

steeple is of stone and rises to a height of 167 feet. The church was built entirely by South Dakota labor, construction being in charge of Leonard J. Eisenman, and most of the general labor was secured from the vicinity of Marty, Ravinia and Wagner. Altogether the edifice is one of which Charles Mix County may well be proud, and no doubt it will become one of the most interesting landmarks in this section as the years go by.

Much of the credit for helpful work must go to the Indian school boys who helped tirelessly in the crushing of stone, wheeling cement, moving lumber, grading, and many other necessary phases of the work. All of the steel scaffolding, hoist tower, etc., was built by the boys and men of the Marty Shops. The Stations of the Cross painted on canvas and hung in niches in the stone walls, are work of one of the art pupils in the Marty High School. Many of the furnishings of the new church are specific donations from loyal friends of the Mission located in various sections of the country, and as they become acquainted with the nature of the work of the Mission their enthusiasm increases. . .

—THE WAGNER POST

CONSECRATION DAY PROCESSION

THE DENVER CATHOLIC REGISTER in a late December 1942 interview, quoted Leonard Eisenman: " . . . In the Marty school shop we fabricated all welded joists, beams, steel balconies, etc., as well as most of the millwork for the school plant, including window sash, doors, frames and screens. Many Marty graduates are making good in the present war effort. . ."

***DIGNITARIES ASSEMBLED ON DECEMBER 17, 1942, AT MARTY
FOR THE CONSECRATION***—*In the center is Bishop William Otterwell
Brady of Sioux Falls. To his left is Abbot Ignatius Esser of St. Meinrad, Indiana.
Next to him is Father Edward Eisenman of Evansville, Indiana, brother of
Father Sylvester. Another brother of Father Sylvester, Father Omer Eisenman
of North Vernon, Indiana, is on the extreme left, bottom row. Opposite him,
bottom row, is Father Cyril Gaul, Master of Ceremonies, St. Meinrad, Indiana.
In the top row (L to R) are Father Boniface who at one time spent about
a year at Marty; Father Leonard Sardo, Franciscan, Pastor of Lake Andes,
South Dakota; Father Timothy Sexton of Marty (behind); Father Justin from
the Crow Creek Reservation; Father Norbert, Headmaster, Marmion Military
Academy; Father Hildebrand, now the Missionary at Turtle Mountains,
formerly of Marty; Father Frank Hulsman, cousin of Father Sylvester, formerly
of Marty and now in charge of the Mission at Winnebago, Nebraska; Father*

Healy of Platte, South Dakota; Father Sylvester of Marty; Father Joseph
Speyer of Chamberlain, South Dakota; Father Isidore Perky of LaPlant, South
Dakota; Father Paul of Fort Totten, North Dakota; Father Rudolph, organist of
St. Meinrad, Indiana; Father Ildephonse, Missionary, Devils Lake Reservation;
Father Willmering, S.J., Missionary to the Potawatomies in Kansas; Father
Drew of Vivian, South Dakota; Father Anselm, Rector of the Major Seminary,
St. Meinrad, Indiana; Father Henry, Chaplain, Benedictine Convent,
Yankton; Father Giesen, Fort Pierre, South Dakota; Father Adelbert, Master of
Ceremonies, Marty; Father Dwerlkotte, Franciscan, Geddes, South Dakota;
Joseph Dieckhaus, Seminarian, and Louis Delahoyde, Seminarian (later
Monsignor). — From January 15, 1943, EYANPAHA KIN, Father Sylvester's
bi-lingual newspaper, also called THE CATHOLIC INDIAN HERALD, sent to
families on three reservations every two weeks.

The Secret Memorial

"When Father Sylvester saw the window showing the Sacrament of the Dying, he had it sent back and changed. The face of the young priest conferring Extreme Unction resembled himself. He wanted no memorial to himself."—Sister Theophane.

His brother Leonard, however, hid a message within the church for future generations to read. Secretly, in the small stair-landing leading up to the choir loft, he inserted into the terrazzo floor a three-inch-diameter plug of plain brass. On it he stamped with his metal punch from the machine shop the letters: "FATHER SYLVESTER AND LEONARD." What a superhuman effort those words represent!

Another Urgent Need: A New Grade School

Not resting from the immense feat of building the church, Marty tackled still another vital task—replacement of the old frame grade school building of 1922. In that December, twenty years back, Father Sylvester bought and wrecked the old Government school building along the Missouri River eight miles south at Greenwood. He hauled the wreckage in his Ford truck to St. Paul's, and built with it St. Therese's Grade School, four classrooms and a basement. It was finished the following year 1923—and after 85 years still finds a use in 2008.

FABRICATING STEEL STAIRS for the new Grade School during acute labor shortage of 1946. Father Ed Eisenman, recovering from a heart attack at his Indiana parish, helps at Marty.

LEONARD AT HIS GRAVEL ELEVATOR

Leonard Falls To His Death

Another urgency was a larger Industrial Arts Building. Leonard produced the blueprints, and was half finished on its construction, at the same time almost completing the new grade school, when tragedy struck. He fell to his death from a scaffold in the new shop building. He was hurrying to inspect steelwork before the bricklayers could continue. That morning, August 21, 1947, exhausted from helping fight prairie fires with wet gunny sacks on several previous nights, Leonard hurried through breakfast. He gazed up from the table a moment toward the heavens and told his wife Josephine, "Some day we will know that it is all worthwhile." In three hours he would know. [He was 54.]

Father Sylvester Follows Within Months

Only six months later, May 26, 1948, Leonard's brother, Father Sylvester, collapsed from overwork and neglect of his own health. He died September 14 in the Benedictine Sisters' Sacred Heart Hospital at Yankton, at age 57. The two builder-brothers were buried in the Marty Cemetery, with Josephine brought back to join them 20 years later. Grandma Elizabeth Hulsman Eisenman lived to age 91. Returning to her two priest sons in Indiana, she carried to the end a weighty correspondence with former Marty families, students, employees and benefactors.

Tribal Council Takes Charge
of School, 1975

After Father Sylvester's death, his fellow monks from St. Meinrad Abbey, Indiana, cared for the school. Then in 1950 they built a branch abbey near Marvin, South Dakota, closer to the Reservation. They honored a wish Father Sylvester expressed before his death, to name it Blue Cloud Abbey for the ardent Yankton chief long insistent on obtaining a Blackrobe and school for the tribe. [For more on Chief Blue Cloud, see *8TH LANDING: THE YANKTON SIOUX MEET LEWIS AND CLARK,* by this author.]

Blue Cloud Abbey in 1975 relinquished governance of the school. The time had come for the Yankton Tribal Council, with Marty graduates filling almost every post, to assume full responsibility for the entire St. Paul's school plant, except for the church and rectory. The latter building became the Motherhouse of the Oblate Sisters of the Blessed Sacrament in 1984.

Badge of Loyalty – Sign-over day in 1975 testified to the strong faith of Marty's early chieftains and their resolute descendants, and to Saint Katharine Drexel's Sisters of the Blessed Sacrament serving at Marty over 60 years. It remains a lasting memorial to the faithful workers, to the unfailing benefactors across America, and to the life's work of Father Sylvester and his brother Leonard.

Apostolate of Oblate Sisters
of The Blessed Sacrament

Through it all, since their founding in 1935, the Oblate Sisters of the Blessed Sacrament have endured. Their ministry of Christ's love reaches even beyond the Yankton Reservation, and especially in loving care of the splendid shrine at Marty dedicated to St. Paul Apostle of the Nations.

OBLATE SISTERS OF THE BLESSED SACRAMENT at Marty in 1948, with Sister Loretta Marie, Sister of the Blessed Sacrament. L to R: Sister Anthony Davis, Sister Timothy (Lillian) Dubois; Sister Christine Hudson, Sister Mary Francis Poitra, Sister Madeleine LeCompte and Sister Inez Jetty.—from 25 SILVER YEARS, Oblate Sisters of the Blessed Sacrament, 1960.

An Aid To Visitors

The steeple piques the interest of travelers for miles around. To aid them, Sister Miriam Shindelar and Sister Inez Jetty produced a 1999 guide, ***BRIEF HISTORY AND SELF-TOUR OF ST. PAUL'S CHURCH,*** an excellent view of this unique shrine, and of Marty's place in history. One note they made on the wealth of symbolism inside the church is a Latin inscription on the stone-facing of the choir loft. It translates: "*O great work of love, death died when Life died upon the cross. Alleluia.*" By whatever designs of Providence, the Feast of the Holy Cross, September 14, was to be the date of Father Sylvester's death in 1948.

Later, in the wake of the1960s Second Vatican Council, Marty added a center altar closer to the congregation.

OBLATE SISTERS OF THE BLESSED SACRAMENT— *L to R, back row: Sr. Miriam Shindelar, Sr. Inez Jetty, Sr. Joan Vittengl, Sr. Patricia Mylott; front row: Sr. Madeleine LeCompte, Sr. Anthony Davis, Sr. Francis Poitra. —OSBS archives.*

SIDE ORATORIES *honor Blessed Kateri Tekakwitha, St. Therese of Lisieux, Our Lady of Guadalupe, The Diving Mercy, and this shrine to St. Katharine Drexel and Father Sylvester, Marty founders.*

THE TEKAKWITHA CONFERENCE of 1500 Catholic Native Americans visits yearly with different tribes across North America as hosts. Centered in Great Falls, Montana. It was founded and chaired by Father Sylvester in 1939.

Now with the shortage of priests in 2008, Marty is fortunate to have as pastor Father David Tickerhoof, T.O.R., Third Order Regular Franciscan from Loretto, Pennsylvania.

The Trees

The trees at Marty now flourish [2008], giants of protection from wind, dust and sun. They were doggedly planted and replanted, literally by the thousands; withered in scorching drought winds, eaten into the ground by descending clouds of ravenous grasshoppers, coaxed year after year with buckets of water carried by everyone, even children. These lofty sentinels stand in salute to the faith of the old

Chiefs, to the early Indian catechists from distant missions, and to the striving of the Yankton parents and their missionaries over these long years . . . .The noble trees surround and embrace, especially, this consecrated link between heaven and earth, the Church of St. Paul Apostle of the Nations.

South of the church stands a distinctive specimen—a stately Ohio Buckeye. A seedling from Kentucky, planted by the Eisenman brothers in the 1930s, it blooms in golden splendor each May in memory of their father, Edward Landelin Eisenman, who was killed at age 31 in a lightning storm in 1895. He left his young widow Elizabeth with four sons under the age of six, destined to team with the Yankton Sioux on their Reservation, building the chiefs' long-held dream of a school and sacred house of worship.

Degree of Perfection

The precision expected in each building detail startled this author on a short home-visit to Leonard and Josephine Eisenman (my Dad and Mother) from my job in Denver in 1942. Dad had just hung the front entrance doors, and those inside dividing the vestibule from the nave. He showed his excitement: "Come over to the job site to see something!!!. . .Put one eye up here to the opening between the two front doors [a tiny slit left for weather-stripping]. Now line this up with the similar slit between the vestibule double doors inside; then squint till you see the sanctuary lamp hanging back [127 feet] at the far end of the nave."

They all aligned exactly on center, a rare achievement controlling the spanning arches. I thought of Dad's ever-present transit. It had done its job. The same ardor of faith and endurance that raised the towering cathedrals around the world worked its purpose in the "Miracle on the Prairie" at Marty, South Dakota.

LEONARD EISENMAN WITH TRANSIT— *Stopped for a moment beside St. Joseph's building in 1937, Leonard Eisenman poses for his daughter with his well-worked transit.—**EFC***

PERFECT CENTER—*From a mark on the walkway outside the High School Building arch, the transit could check center line on mortar joints all the way up the distant church building, including the center of the cross.*

"A House of God as fitting for divine worship as human hands can make it."--Historian Sister M. Claudia Duratschek, O.S.B., in her *CRUSADING ALONG SIOUX TRAILS. 1947.*

VIRGIN PRAIRIE SOD SURROUND—*To stabilize the fill-dirt around the new church, Father Sylvester and crew carefully dug and carried*

*slabs of virgin prairie sod, the toughest of barriers against erosion---
Mother Earth's circle of protection around the house of God. —EFC*

THE CHURCH OF ST. PAUL THE APOSTLE attracts pilgrimages from afar, as well as local Reservation and outlying families, to this sacred

place. North of the church stands St. Sylvester's Convent, since 1984 the motherhouse of the Oblate Sisters of the Blessed Sacrament.

MIRACLE ON THE PRAIRIE 75

Through the decades, many graduates have worked long and faithfully at Marty. Generations have served generously in Tribal posts, from chairman on down. A pioneer in the Deaconate Program of the Sioux Falls Diocese is Edward Zephier, Jr., a grandson of the noted emissary David Zephier who went in quest of Father Sylvester in 1921. Ed has ministered to the spiritual needs of the Yanktons.

Loyal employees of Father Sylvester's day, as well, persevered for years in the Marty spirit with their devotion to the school and Reservation. This author, beginning in 1975, traveled the U. S. to interview some of these retirees, as well as Reservation families, in their final years, for memories to include in this and three earlier books.

THE MOTHER LODE, TO HISTORIANS, is the personal letter— handwritten, the better. Fortunately, the eldest Eisenman brother Omer, in 1941 pastor of St. Mary's Parish, North Vernon, Indiana, had been saving all family correspondence since 1906. In the year 1941, however, because of the building rush, only two came from Leonard's pen. But he often stayed up late at night to write his three faraway children literally working their way through college. Pressing hard through three sheets of carbon, tightly cramping the margins, Leonard shared the human and mechanical details of his labor on the church. Under the happy title THE POPSIE BUGLE, these precious onion-skin relics, ironically, did not survive. A heavy burden of regret can haunt one who fails to save priceless documents. [For one search that did pay off, see Appendix No. 7, page 83.]

The END

CHRONOLOGY

St. Paul Apostle of The Nations Church
Marty, South Dakota

1866 – Five Yankton Sioux chiefs petition U.S. Government for school and Blackrobe.

1879 – Yanktons build St. Ann's school, Whetstone. Chalkrock building crumbles.

October 22, 1913 –First St. Paul Chapel built by Fr. Henry Westropp, S.J., working out of Pine Ridge.

November 1914 to March 1916 – Father Westropp serves St. Paul congregation, lives a year in tiny sacristy, until assigned to India.

December 1917 to September 1918 – Fr. Ambrose Mattingly, O.S.B., from Immaculate Conception Mission, Stephan, covers St. Paul's on a ten-station circuit monthly out of Stephan.

1918-1922 – Fr. Sylvester Eisenman, O.S.B., takes over the circuit. Old church from Wagner, SD, hauled over prairie to site of St. Paul's Chapel. Readied for use in 1922.

1921 – Three Yankton elders journey to Indiana and secure Father Sylvester as their permanent pastor.

March 5, 1941 – Old 1918 church vacated and razed in one week. Lumber saved for concrete forms on new church.

April 5, 1941 – Father Sylvester pushes first wheelbarrow concrete down the ramp for column footings.

May 2, 1941 – First section concrete wall completed.

May 25, 1941 – Cornerstone laid.

[July 24, 1941 – 114 degrees in the shade.]

August 5, 1941 – Basement slab poured, 750 sacks of cement this day.

Nov. 14, 1941 – Two more arches go up.

February 8, 1942 – Steel elevator shaft erected to lift concrete into pillar forms.

March 24, 1942 – Final slab poured in one piece.

April 14, 1942 – Cross placed on steeple.

April 20, 1942 – Two large bells hoisted to belfry.

August 16, 1942 – Final arch out of danger.

December 17, 1942 – FINISH – Consecration ceremony held.

CHURCH DIMENSIONS AND MATERIALS

Height - 167 feet

Interior length of nave - 127 feet

Seating capacity- 650

Exterior - Indiana limestone (Bedford)

Interior - St. Meinrad, Indiana, sandstone

Flooring - Terrazzo

Interior décor - Native Indian design

From southern Indiana stone quarries, soft shades of golden sand, pale orchid and umber, spread across the arching pillars and walls,literally exposing sands walked by ancestors in ages past.

PRINCIPAL CONSTRUCTORS AND ARTISANS

Architect: Paul Schulte, Cincinnati, OH.

Builder: Leonard John Eisenman, Sr., Marty, SD.

Labor foreman: John Doty, Ravinia, SD.

Stained Glass Windows: Emil Frei, St. Louis, MO.

Mural behind altar: Mr. & Mrs. Zimmerman of Cincinnati, OH.

Bells: Stuckstede Co., St. Louis, MO.

Stations of the Cross: Oils by Cecilia Grinnell,
    of Elbowoods, ND, senior at St. Paul High School.

Railings, pews and doors by High School boys in Marty
    carpenter shop.

Steelwork by High School boys in Marty machine shop.

Roofing: Ralph Tessier of Mitchell, SD.

Plumbing: A. B. Vinatieri of Yankton, SD.

Plastering: Matt Thome of Yankton.

Electricians: Leonard "Shorty" Battin and Frank Kohoutek of Yankton.

Stonemasons: Gus and Henry Morgen of Yankton.

Hauling and crushing rock and sand: School boys and girls,
    seminarians and other Marty folk.

APPENDIX

No 1 - Text of Historical Marker, page 2

MARTIN MARTY 1834-1896

First Abbot of St. Meinrad Archabbey. First Bishop of the Dakota Territory, began to visit the Indians in this territory in 1877. He established the first Indian Mission called St. Ann's Mission at Wheeler, about 30 miles N.W. of here in 1878. The same year South Dakota was  created a State, 1889, he was made the first Bishop of Sioux Falls, South Dakota.

REV. SYLVESTER EISENMAN 1892 [should be 1891] - 1948

With the help of many friends, built St. Paul's Mission, Marty, and with the aid of 3 Blessed Sacrament Sisters he opened it as a School for Indian Education in 1924. In 1935 he established here the Convent for the Oblate Sisters of the Blessed Sacrament. He laid down his burden on the Feast of the Exaltation of the Holy Cross September 14, 1948.

Visitors are welcome.

No. 2 - The West Farm, page 15.

At a mile west and ¼ mile north of the Mission, the West Farm corralled the beef herd. The white-faced Herefords watered there at the round tank beneath the clapping windmill. Vital, they put food on the table at Marty. This author's family, in 1930, moved to the acreage and its bungalow, lost by a young farmer in the raging Depression

the year before. Too young to know that sad tale, we children had adventures galore: On a bitter cold Sunday January 3, 1937, we returned from Mass. Dad was away on business. Fourteen-year-old brother Ed went to check the barnyard. He loved the cattle. My diary says: "We all struggled for life and death to rescue a big cow [actually it was an 800-lb. steer] from drowning in the icy water tank. Through the lid opening of one sq. yd. we kept the poor creature's head out of water, kneeling on the slippery ramp of ice [from the dripping mouths], all drenched and exhausted, before Joe Sanders and Louie Votava arrived from the main farm with a team." All night in the barn everyone fought to save the steer. Grandma Eisenman brought up whiskey and more blankets. To no avail. [Forever, those pleading eyes, the strong breath and our slipping grab around his neck will haunt this author.]

No. 3 - The Dairy Farm, page 15.

On a slight rise across Mosquito Creek west of the Mission rose the big dairy barn. People took bottles to the Separator Room for milk and cream. The school boys had many escapades at the farm, many of them kept untold, such as riding the purebred Holstein calves—forbidden pleasure. Also milking was only one of the skills rotated for them, such as print shop, bakery, machine and carpenter shop, and shoe repair. Plenty of shoes, as almost all came from a second round of feet before landing in the Parcel Post room. Equal experience opened for the girls. The little ones invented "run and slide" on thick cloths to polish the floors. Kitchen, laundry, infirmary, office, and Parcel Post room offered experience. Recreation filled another whole category.

No. 4 – The Builder-seminarians, page 27.

Marty's summer seminarian volunteers of the 1940s followed noble footsteps: in the early 1820s, young Pierre-Jean DeSmet, S.J. (from Belgium), carried bricks to build a school for American Indian boys (Iowa, Sauk, Menominee and Osage) in Missouri. It grew to be St. Louis University. Then in 1839 Father DeSmet ascended the Missouri River by steamboat to visit the Yankton Sioux, answering appeals from the Western tribes.

No. 5 –Toll on the Automobiles, page 40.

On that desperate drive to Wagner with Ray Flying Hawk and the rattlesnake bite, my Mother matched any Indianapolis-500 driver, but not on a smooth track. The six miles to the State highway went ungraveled until about 1937. Our supper table bristled with repeated debate between Dad and the three boys. If not on trucks, it was Ford over Chevrolet. The Chevys had stronger bodies and less rattles, but Fords had clearance in the mud and snow—and they would start in winter. Road misery claimed a Ford a year.

No. 6 – Leonard's missing violin fingers, page 42.

Trying out a motorcycle he repaired for a veteran returning to Indiana after World War I., in 1919, Leonard's left hand lost all but thumb, index finger, and half the middle finger. Marty workmen said it never made Leonard hesitate to climb the narrow rungs of frozen water tank nor to lift heavy loads. Shortly before his death, he oversaw building of looms and classroom interior for an accredited Arts and Crafts department. His second daughter Angela, college degree in hand, filled Father Sylvester's plan to research and set up a certified curriculum. The Oblate Sisters and others then carried the work forward to national acclaim.

No. 7 – Search for the Ironworker, page 76.

Proving the truth of a long-held tale is no small triumph for the historian. It is a real joy. In this writer's years of research, mainly on the Yankton Sioux people at Marty, one case stands out. All through the years, my Grandmother Elizabeth Hulsman Eisenman, who died at 91, told us a magical tale. It was that Grandpa, taken from this life at age 31, had worked for Snead Iron Works of Louisville on the ornamental ironwork of the Library of Congress in Washington, D.C., and also on the famous Old Boston Public Library. Outlandish claim it was, for a firm in Kentucky. But by real detective work–and luck–we found in the inner sanctum vaults of the Boston Public an 1895 booklet. It sketched the intricate ironwork inside and out, as well as the stacks, credited to Snead & Co. Iron Works of Louisville! It should have been no surprise—Eisenman means "Iron Man," from the Bavarian Ironworker Guilds of old.

No. 8 – The Grand Mural in the Sanctuary (cover)

Francis Bernie wrote a descripion of the grand mural, with a five-column photo in the *Wagner Post*, October 9, 1991:

The theme, "Heaven and the Roads to Heaven" depicts also Native American Indian figures.

Top center—Figure of God the Father enthroned in majesty and glory——surrounded by cherubim——in flame color to express the radiance of God.

Below—The dove or the Holy Spirit——the seven rays, Tongues of Flame, or the seven gifts of the Holy Spirit descending through the crucifixion to all on earth.

To the right and left of the dove—two figures of the great Archangels,

Michael and Gabriel. Michael on the left in armor and sword holding the scales of judgment. Gabriel, the angel of the Annunciation, holding lily.

On the right hand of God the Father—The Blessed Mother seated and crowned as Queen of Heaven, in attitude interceding for humanity; St. John close to her as her son, holds book as one of the evangelists; St. Joseph holds lily symbolizing protection of Mary; the boy martyr Tarcisius, as a server, holds napkin as symbol of his death, killed delivering the wafers of Holy Communion; St. Peter with keys; St. Mark with book as evangelist; St. Andrew with "X" cross, attribute of death; St. James the Great, shell and pilgrim's staff; St. Benedict with crosier, as founder of Benedictine order; St. Maurus and St. Placid with Indian boys showing great influence and service of the order to the present day; St. Scholastica with crosier, foundress of order; Anonymous Indians.

Below Tarcisius— St. Norbert holding monstrance traditional symbol of his interests; behind him, anonymous figure; St. Gregory the Great, Pope receiving spirit of the Holy Spirit as shown by the bird at rear; St. Dominic with rosary; St. Pascal Boylan, Franciscan; St. Francis Xavier as missionary priest carrying the message of God; St. Charles Borromeo, rope around neck, the Hangman's noose, that broke; St. Anthony with Lily.

Below St. Dominic— St. Rose of Lima, crown of roses; Cure of Ars, as village priest.

Next across— St. Clare with monstrance, symbolizing the time she held back the Tartars with the host; St. Francis de Sales with quill and book indicating his great writings; St. Genevieve with lighted candle; anonymous figure; King with Shield with Black Eagle; St. Wenceslaus; below and all above: singing and adoring angels.

Right side at top— St. John the Baptist with reed cross and banner "Behold the Lamb of God;" St. Bartholomew with knife and attribute of martyrdom; St. Matthew as apostle and evangelist; St. Thomas with building square.

Below St. John— Blessed Imelda; St. Ignatius; St. Aloysius with lily; St. Francis with stigmata; anonymous Sisters and Indian Girls and Indian men.

Below St. Ignatius— St. Thomas Aquinas with book and quill to express his writings; St. Therese, Little Flower; behind her anonymous figure; [Blessed] Katherine Tekakwitha; St. Patrick as bishop holding three-leaf shamrock; St. Vincent de Paul holding infant as protector of foundlings.

Below St. Thomas— St. Gertrude: St. Benedict Joseph Labre with rosary around neck and hands; the tramp of the Blessed Sacrament; St. Margaret Mary displaying picture of Sacred Heart; Franciscan Phillip of Jesus; St. Sylvester in blue with staff as founder of the Sylvesterines; St. Louis; and St. Blanche holding flowers as symbol of responsibility and trust. Below all and above, the choir of singing and adoring angels.

Bottom left— St. Elizabeth feeding the poor; St. Isidore as patron of labor; St. Cecilia with musical instrument as patron of music; St. Lawrence holding Gospel and gridiron attribute of martyrdom.

Bottom right— St. Stephen; St. Agnes; St. Martin of Tours; Saints Augustine and Monica; anonymous Sister of the Blessed Sacrament and Oblate Sister of the Blessed Sacrament, and Indian Child.

In the foreground, Creatures of the Prairie drinking from the River of Life.

About the Author

From a heart touched by an ancient culture, after life on the Yankton Sioux Reservation from age ten, this author presents her fourth book on the South Dakota tribe. Her parents moved from Indiana to assist at Marty. She studied at Loretto Heights College , Denver, Colorado; University of Wyoming, Boise State University, and Universidad de Santo Domingo in the Caribbean while her husband William served there with the U. S. State Department, and later in Bolivia. A native of Indianapolis, Indiana, mother of four, she taught English in Latin America, and Spanish stateside. She now resides in Seattle, Washington.